The War Poems

Isaac Rosenberg

CONTENTS

Introduction

Isaac Rosenberg (1890 - 1918) occupies a strange position in English poetry, it seems to me. There is general agreement in academic circles that his war poems are amongst the finest produced by any writer in English in response to the horrors of war in the trenches of the Western Front. At the same time, his work is not as well known by the general public (if at all) as the work of poets such as Owen and Sassoon. One of the purposes of this edition of his poetry is to make available to the reading public a cheap print edition of Rosenberg's war poems. I have chosen not to include any extracts from Rosenberg's journal nor his two unfinished plays: these might be of interest to the academic or to the committed enthusiast, but if Rosenberg is to become better known as a great poet of the First World War, then it is the poems that must speak for him. This edition deliberately omits Rosenberg's pre-war poetry, so that readers of this edition can concentrate on the war poems.

The literary critic Irving Howe commented on Rosenberg:

The early Rosenberg is always driving himself to say more than he has to say, because he thinks poets must speak to large matters. Later he learns that in a poppy in the trenches or a louse in a soldier's shirt, there is enough matter for poetry.

Unlike Sassoon in particular whose early poems about the war are extremely positive, Rosenberg was critical of the war from the outset and, quite apart from the inherent qualities of his poetry, his perspective is unique amongst poets of the First World War: he was working class, Jewish and had not been to public school, and so from the first he did not approach the war from the jingoistic perspective of a member of the privileged Edwardian gentleman class.

Perhaps it is his unconventional background (unconventional only in the sense that it was so different from most poets of the time) that gives some of his poetry the qualities of compassion and tenderness combined with cynicism and humour – qualities perhaps which led

Paul Fussell to claim that 'Break of Day in the Trenches' is "the greatest poem of the war."

Certainly that poem along with 'Returning, We Hear the Larks', 'Dead Man's Dump', 'In the Trenches' and 'Louse Hunting' are at least equal in depth and emotional impact as well as verbal dexterity to anything written by Wilfred Owen, and, along with 'Break of Day in the Trenches', they deserve to be more widely known and admired.

A Worm Fed on the Heart of Corinth

A worm fed on the heart of Corinth,
Babylon and Rome:
Not Paris raped tall Helen,
But this incestuous worm,
Who lured her vivid beauty
To his amorphous sleep.
England! Famous as Helen
Is thy betrothal sung
To him the shadowless,
More amorous than Solomon.

Daughters of War

Space beats the ruddy freedom of their limbs,
Their naked dances with man's spirit naked
By the root side of the tree of life
(The underside of things
And shut from earth's profoundest eyes).

I saw in prophetic gleams
These mighty daughters in their dances
Beckon each soul aghast from its crimson corpse
To mix in their glittering dances:
I heard the mighty daughters' giant sighs
In sleepless passion for the sons of valour
And envy of the days of flesh,
Barring their love with mortal boughs across-
The mortal boughs, the mortal tree of life.
The old bark burnt with iron wars
They blow to a live flame
To char the young green clays
And reach the occult soul; they have no softer lure,
No softer lure than the savage ways of death.

We were satisfied of our lords the moon and the sun
To take our wage of sleep and bread and warmth -
These maidens came-these strong ever-living Amazons,
And in an easy might their wrists
Of night's sway and noon's sway the sceptres brake,
Clouding the wild, the soft lustres of our eyes.

Clouding the wild lustres, the clinging tender lights;
Driving the darkness into the flame of clay
With the Amazonian wind of them
Over our corroding faces
That must be broken-broken for evermore,
So the soul can leap out
Into their huge embraces,
Though there are human faces
Best sculptures of Deity,
And sinews lusted after
By the Archangels tall,
Even these must leap to the love-heat of these maidens
From the flame of terrene days,
Leaving grey ashes to the wind-to the wind.

One (whose great lifted face,
Where wisdom's strength and beauty's strength
And the thewed strength of large beasts
Moved and merged, gloomed and lit)
Was speaking, surely, as the earth-men's earth fell away;
Whose new hearing drank the sound
Where pictures, lutes, and mountains mixed
With the loosed spirit of a thought,

Essenced to language thus

'My sisters force their males
From the doomed earth, from the doomed glee
And hankering of hearts.
Frail hands gleam up through the human quagmire, and lips

of ash
Seem to wail, as in sad faded paintings
Far-sunken and strange.
My sisters have their males
Clean of the dust of old days
That clings about those white hands
And yearns in those voices sad:
But these shall not see them,
Or think of them in any days or years;
They are my sisters' lovers in other days and years.'

August 1914

What in our lives is burnt
In the fire of this?
The heart's dear granary?
The much we shall miss?

Three lives hath one life -
Iron, honey, gold.
The gold, the honey gone -
Left is the hard and cold.

Iron are our lives
Molten right through our youth.
A burnt space through ripe fields
A fair mouth's broken tooth.

On Receiving News of the War

Snow is a strange white word.
No ice or frost
Has asked of bud or bird
For Winter's cost.

Yet ice and frost and snow
From earth to sky
This Summer land doth know.
No man knows why.

In all men's hearts it is.
Some spirit old
Hath turned with malign kiss
Our lives to mould.

Red fangs have torn His face.
God's blood is shed.
He mourns from His lone place
His children dead.

O! ancient crimson curse!
Corrode, consume.
Give back this universe
Its pristine bloom.

Lusitania

Chaos! that coincides with this militant purpose.

Chaos! the heart of this earnest malignancy.

Chaos! that helps, chaos that gives to shatter

Mind-wrought, mind-unimagining energies

For topless ill, of dynamite and iron.

Soulless logic, inventive enginery.

Now you have got the peace-faring Lusitania,

Germany's gift - all earth they would give thee, Chaos.

The Troop Ship

Grotesque and queerly huddled
Contortionists to twist
The sleepy soul to a sleep,
We lie all sorts of ways
And cannot sleep.
The wet wind is so cold,
And the lurching men so careless,
That, should you drop to a doze,
Winds' fumble or men's feet
Are on your face.

Marching

(As Seen from the Left File)

My eyes catch ruddy necks
Sturdily pressed back -
All a red brick moving glint.
Like flaming pendulums, hands
Swing across the khaki -
Mustard-coloured khaki -
To the automatic feet.
We husband the ancient glory
In these bared necks and hands.
Not broke is the forge of Mars;
But a subtler brain beats iron
To shoe the hoofs of death,
(Who paws dynamic air now).
Blind fingers loose an iron cloud
To rain immortal darkness
On strong eyes.

Break of Day in the Trenches

The darkness crumbles away.
It is the same old druid Time as ever,
Only a live thing leaps my hand,
A queer sardonic rat,
As I pull the parapet's poppy
To stick behind my ear.
Droll rat, they would shoot you if they knew
Your cosmopolitan sympathies,
Now you have touched this English hand
You will do the same to a German
Soon, no doubt, if it be your pleasure
To cross the sleeping green between.
It seems you inwardly grin as you pass
Strong eyes, fine limbs, haughty athletes,
Less chanced than you for life,
Bonds to the whims of murder,
Sprawled in the bowels of the earth,
The torn fields of France.
What do you see in our eyes
At the shrieking iron and flame
Hurled through still heavens?
What quaver - what heart aghast?
Poppies whose roots are in men's veins
Drop, and are ever dropping;
But mine in my ear is safe,
Just a little white with the dust.

Killed In Action

Your 'Youth' has fallen from its shelf,
And you have fallen, you yourself.
They knocked a soldier on the head,
I mourn the poet who fell dead.
And yet I think it was by chance,
By oversight you died in France.
You were so poor an outward man,
So small against your spirit's span,
That Nature, being tired awhile,
Saw but your outward human pile;
And Nature, who would never let
A sun with light still in it set,
Before you even reached your sky,
In inadvertence let you die.

Wan, Fragile Faces of Joy!

Wan, fragile faces of joy!
Pitiful mouths that strive
To light with smiles the place
We dream we walk alive.

To you I stretch my hands;
Hands shut in pitiless trance
In a land of ruin and woe,
The desolate land of France.

Dear faces, startled and shaken,
Out of wild dust and sounds,
You yearn to me, lure and sadden
My heart with futile bounds.

From France

The spirit drank the Café lights;
All the hot life that glittered there,
And heard men say to women gay,
'Life is just so in France'.

The spirit dreams of Café lights,
And golden faces and soft tones,
And hears men groan to broken men,
'This is not Life in France'.

Heaped stones and a charred signboard shows
With grass between and dead folk under,
And some birds sing, while the spirit takes wing.
And this is life in France.

In the Trenches

I snatched two poppies
From the parapet's ledge,
Two bright red poppies
That winked on the ledge.
Behind my ear
I stuck one through,
One blood red poppy
I gave to you.

The sandbags narrowed
And screwed out our jest,
And tore the poppy
You had on your breast...
Down - a shell - O! Christ,
I am choked... safe... dust blind, I
See trench floor poppies
Strewn. Smashed you lie.

Returning, We Hear the Larks

Sombre the night is.
And though we have our lives, we know
What sinister threat lies there.

Dragging these anguished limbs, we only know
This poison-blasted track opens on our camp -
On a little safe sleep.

But hark! joy - joy - strange joy.
Lo! heights of night ringing with unseen larks.
Music showering our upturned list'ning faces.

Death could drop from the dark
As easily as song -
But song only dropped,
Like a blind man's dreams on the sand
By dangerous tides,
Like a girl's dark hair for she dreams no ruin lies there,
Or her kisses where a serpent hides.

The Destruction of Jerusalem by the Babylonian Hordes

They left their Babylon bare
Of all its tall men,
Of all its proud horses;
They made for Lebanon.

And shadowy sowers went
Before their spears to sow
The fruit whose taste is ash,
For Judah's soul to know.

They who bowed to the Bull god,
Whose wings roofed Babylon,
In endless hosts darkened
The bright-heavened Lebanon.

They washed their grime in pools
Where laughing girls forgot
The wiles they used for Solomon.
Sweet laughter, remembered not!

Sweet laughter charred in the flame
That clutched the cloud and earth,
While Solomon's towers crashed between
To a gird of Babylon's mirth.

The Burning of the Temple

Fierce wrath of Solomon,
Where sleepest thou?
O see, the fabric which thou won
Earth and ocean to give thee-
O look at the red skies.

Or hath the sun plunged down?
What is this molten gold -
These thundering fires blown
Through heaven, where the smoke rolled?
Again the great king dies.

His dreams go out in smoke.
His days he let not pass
And sculptured here are broke,
Are charred as the burnt grass,
Gone as his mouth's last sighs.

Significance

The cunning moment curves its claws
Round the body of our curious wish
But push a shoulder through its straitened laws
Then are you hooked to wriggle like a fish.

Lean in high middle 'twixt two tapering points,
Yet rocks and undulations control
The agile brain the limber joints
The sinews of the soul.

Chaos that coincides, form that refutes all sway,
Shapes to the eye quite other to the touch,
All twisted things continue to our clay
Like added limbs and hair dispreaded overmuch.

And after it draws in its claws
The rocks and unquiet sink to a flat ground,
Then follow desert-hours, the vacuous pause
Till some mad indignation unleashes the hound.

And those flat hours and dead unseeing things

Cower and crowd and burrow for us to use

Where sundry gapings spurn and preparing wings

And O! our hands would use all ere we lose.

Home-Thoughts from France

Wan, fragile faces of joy,
Pitiful mouths that strive
To light with smiles the place
We dream we walk alive,

To you I stretch my hands,
Hands shut in pitiless trance
In a land of ruin and woe,
The desolate land of France.

Dear faces startled and shaken,
Out of wild dust and sounds
You yearn to me, lure and sadden
My heart with futile bounds.

In War

Fret the nonchalant noon
With your spleen
Or your gay brow,
For the motion of your spirit
Ever moves with these.

When day shall be too quiet,
Deaf to you
And your dumb smile,
Untuned air shall lap the stillness
In the old space for your voice -

The voice that once could mirror
Remote depths
Of moving being,
Stirred by responsive voices near,
Suddenly stilled for ever.

No ghost darkens the places
Dark to One;
But my eyes dream,
And my heart is heavy to think
How it was heavy once.

In the old days when death Stalked the world
For the flower of men,
And the rose of beauty faded
And pined in the great gloom,

One day we dug a grave:
We were vexed
With the sun's heat.
We scanned the hooded dead:
At noon we sat and talked.

How death had kissed their eyes
Three dread noons since,
How human art won
The dark soul to flicker
Till it was lost again:

And we whom chance kept whole-
But haggard,
Spent-were charged
To make a place for them who knew
No pain in any place.

The good priest came to pray;
Our ears half heard,
And half we thought
Of alien things, irrelevant;
And the heat and thirst were great.

The good priest read: 'I heard.
Dimly my brain
Held words and lost....
Sudden my blood ran cold....

God! God! It could not be.

He read my brother's name; I sank-
I clutched the priest.
They did not tell me it was he
Was killed three days ago.

What are the great sceptred dooms
To us, caught
In the wild wave
We break ourselves on them,
My brother, our hearts and years.

The Immortals

I killed them, but they would not die.
Yea! all the day and all the night
For them I could not rest or sleep,
Nor guard from them nor hide in flight.

Then in my agony I turned
And made my hands red in their gore.
In vain - for faster than I slew
They rose more cruel than before.

I killed and killed with slaughter mad;
I killed till all my strength was gone.
And still they rose to torture me,
For Devils only die in fun.

I used to think the Devil hid
In women's smiles and wine's carouse.
I called him Satan, Beelzebub.
But now I call him, dirty louse.

Louse Hunting

Nudes - stark and glistening,
Yelling in lurid glee. Grinning faces
And raging limbs
Whirl over the floor one fire.
For a shirt verminously busy
Yon soldier tore from his throat, with oaths
Godhead might shrink at, but not the lice.
And soon the shirt was aflare
Over the candle he'd lit while we lay.

Then we all sprang up and stript
To hunt the verminous brood.
Soon like a demons' pantomine
The place was raging.
See the silhouettes agape,
See the glibbering shadows
Mixed with the battled arms on the wall.
See gargantuan hooked fingers
Pluck in supreme flesh
To smutch supreme littleness.
See the merry limbs in hot Highland fling
Because some wizard vermin
Charmed from the quiet this revel
When our ears were half lulled
By the dark music
Blown from Sleep's trumpet.

Girl to a Soldier on Leave

Love! You love me - your eyes
Have looked through death at mine.
You have tempted a grave too much
I let you - I repine.

I love you - Titan lover,
My own storm-days Titan.
Greater than the son of Zeus,
I know whom I would choose.

Titan - my splendid rebel -
The old Prometheus
Wanes like a ghost before your power -
His pangs were joys to yours.

Pallid days arid and wan
Tied your soul fast.
Babel-cities smoky tops
Pressed upon your growth

Weary gyves. What were you
But a word in the brains ways,
Or the sleep of Circes swine.
One gyve holds you yet.

It held you hiddenly on the Somme
Tied from my heart at home.
O must it loosen now? - I wish

You were bound with the old gyves.

Love! you love me - your eyes
Have looked through death at mine.
You have tempted a grave too much.
I let you - I repine.

Soldier: Twentieth Century

I love you, great new Titan!
Am I not you?
Napoleon or Caesar
Out of you grew.

Out of the unthinkable torture,
Eyes kissed by death,
Won back to the world again,
Lost and won in a breath,

Cruel men are made immortal,
Out of your pain born.
They have stolen the sun's power
With their feet on your shoulders worn.

Let them shrink from your girth,
That has outgrown the pallid days,
When you slept like Circe's swine,
Or a word in the brain's way.

The Jew

Moses, from whose loins I sprung,
Lit by a lamp in his blood
Ten immutable rules, a moon
For mutable lampless men.

The blonde, the bronze, the ruddy,
With the same heaving blood,
Keep tide to the moon of Moses.
Then why do they sneer at me?

Spring, 1916

Slow, rigid, is this masquerade
That passes as through a difficult air:
Heavily-heavily passes.
What has she fed on? Who her table laid
Through the three seasons? What forbidden fare
Ruined her as a mortal lass is?

I played with her two years ago,
Who might be now her own sister in stone;
So altered from her May mien,
When round the pink a necklace of warm snow
Laughed to her throat where my mouth's touch had gone.
How is this, ruined Queen?

Who lured her vivid beauty so
To be that strained chill thing that moves
So ghastly midst her young brood
Of pregnant shoots that she for men did grow?
Where are the strong men who made these their loves?
Spring! God pity your mood!

The Dying Soldier

'Here are houses,' he moaned,
'I could reach, but my brain swims.'
Then they thundered and flashed,
And shook the earth to its rims.

'They are gunpits,' he gasped,
'Our men are at the guns.
Water!... Water!... Oh, water!
For one of England's dying sons.'

'We cannot give you water,
Were all England in your breath.'
'Water!.... Water! …. Oh, water!'
He moaned and swooned to death.

Dead Man's Dump

The plunging limbers over the shattered track
Racketed with their rusty freight,
Stuck out like many crowns of thorns,
And the rusty stakes like sceptres old
To stay the flood of brutish men
Upon our brothers dear.

The wheels lurched over sprawled dead
But pained them not, though their bones crunched,
Their shut mouths made no moan.
They lie there huddled, friend and foeman,
Man born of man, and born of woman,
And shells go crying over them
From night till night and now.

Earth has waited for them,
All the time of their growth
Fretting for their decay:
Now she has them at last!
In the strength of their strength
Suspended - stopped and held.

What fierce imaginings their dark souls lit?
Earth! have they gone into you!
Somewhere they must have gone,
And flung on your hard back
Is their soul's sack
Emptied of God-ancestralled essences.

Who hurled them out? Who hurled?

None saw their spirits' shadow shake the grass,
Or stood aside for the half used life to pass
Out of those doomed nostrils and the doomed mouth,
When the swift iron burning bee
Drained the wild honey of their youth.

What of us who, flung on the shrieking pyre,
Walk, our usual thoughts untouched,
Our lucky limbs as on ichor fed,
Immortal seeming ever?
Perhaps when the flames beat loud on us,
A fear may choke in our veins
And the startled blood may stop.

The air is loud with death,
The dark air spurts with fire,
The explosions ceaseless are.
Timelessly now, some minutes past,
Those dead strode time with vigorous life,
Till the shrapnel called 'An end!'
But not to all. In bleeding pangs
Some borne on stretchers dreamed of home,
Dear things, war-blotted from their hearts.

Maniac Earth! howling and flying, your bowel
Seared by the jagged fire, the iron love,
The impetuous storm of savage love.

Dark Earth! dark Heavens! swinging in chemic smoke,
What dead are born when you kiss each soundless soul
With lightning and thunder from your mined heart,
Which man's self-dug, and his blind fingers loosed?

A man's brains splattered on
A stretcher-bearer's face;
His shook shoulders slipped their load,
But when they bent to look again
The drowning soul was sunk too deep
For human tenderness.

They left this dead with the older dead,
Stretched at the cross roads.

Burnt black by strange decay
Their sinister faces lie,
The lid over each eye,
The grass and coloured clay
More motion have than they,
Joined to the great sunk silences.

Here is one not long dead;
His dark hearing caught our far wheels,
And the choked soul stretched weak hands
To reach the living word the far wheels said,
The blood-dazed intelligence beating for light,
Crying through the suspense of the far torturing wheels
Swift for the end to break

Or the wheels to break,
Cried as the tide of the world broke over his sight.

Will they come? Will they ever come?
Even as the mixed hoofs of the mules,
The quivering-bellied mules,
And the rushing wheels all mixed
With his tortured upturned sight.
So we crashed round the bend,
We heard his weak scream,
We heard his very last sound,
And our wheels grazed his dead face.

The Dead Heroes

Flame out, you glorious skies,
Welcome our brave;
Kiss their exultant eyes;
Give what they gave.

Flash, mailed seraphim,
Your burning spears;
New days to outflame their dim
Heroic years.

Thrills their baptismal tread
The bright proud air;
The embattled plumes outspread
Burn upwards there.

Flame out, flame out, O Song!
Star ring to star;
Strong as our hurt is strong
Our children are.

Their blood is England's heart;
By their dead hands
It is their noble part
That England stands.

England-Time gave them thee;
They gave back this

To win Eternity
And claim God's kiss.

Printed in Great Britain
by Amazon

36055825R00030